# The Smokey Lounge

Jose Gabriel Garcia

authorHOUSE®

AuthorHouse™
1663 Liberty Drive
Bloomington, IN 47403
www.authorhouse.com
Phone: 1 (800) 839-8640

Published by AuthorHouse    05/22/2015

ISBN: 978-1-5049-1246-4 (sc)
ISBN: 978-1-5049-1247-1 (e)

Library of Congress Control Number: 2015907969

Print information available on the last page.

Any people depicted in stock imagery provided by Thinkstock are models, and
such images are being used for illustrative purposes only.
Certain stock imagery © Thinkstock.

This book is printed on acid-free paper.

# Table of Contents

# Sparkling Comet

Champaigning in my
Sparkling floating comet
nearly offended
Though not
as to even
with a reflecting image
Of a giant glass-top floor
Of the Empire State Building-
Then, you're coolin' and the gang.
Ha! Such lusciousness.
The city that never sleeps..
It is so nice
That insomnia sounds inviting.
Then, that's another story to be timely told.

## Rasta Lingo

I am but a speck of a speck
In the cosmos of God.
So respec'!

# Through the Crowds and Convenience Stores

The deaf stares from those attractive, is cruel.

They walk as if

The burning desire never existed..

It is insulting to be absolutely denied by the half dressed

Simultaneously playing a part, in the emotionally

sympathetic marathon of the moving masses.

Being.

Looking.

Having. And nothing.

# Billár

..Dos mingo

Un Domingo en la sala

En una mesa de billár.

El mingo le dió a la bola amarilla,

Que rebotó al segúndo mingo

Al comenzár de una noche larga y sin hora,

Guapamente sobrio con una brillante vista inegable a la ciudád viva

En el pueblo particular y a la ves,

un sentimiento de bienvenidos; ¡disfrutándo su recreo!

# Father Time

To briefly branch out of the
Every day routine, in the name of love,
With a meaningful argument
And, even if the conversation sours
to never see that person
Ever; Hang tough..
At least you have time.

# Prayer Candles On Line

Prayer candles in the

line of service

a prideful, automatomical, envious,

and egotistical march.

Time allotted to this rotten repugnant venomous reprisals

As civil as the utter whimsicalness being silently clamorous

Relentlessly watching paint dry modernly I suppose.

Their agenda continues

Ahead of the commoner;

Not even starved animals folks!

Be it what it is

Living well is the best revenge

And if the writers opinion be permitted..

If it came around for me to hand down

justice at an all to one,

I'd put all those parasites

in one bag

directly sent gasoline-rocket nitro to

the Sun! swarming sonsofbitches.

# Velónes en la Fila

Velónes en la
Fila de servicio
una marcha
celóza, automatomica, orgulloza y
egoísta.
Tiempo asignando al repugnánte represalia corrumpído.
Civil, hací a lo errático clamorosamente en su propio siléncio.
Perésa modernamente sin tregua, supóngo.
Sus agendas pragmático acertíjos
un paso alante las masas y obreros;
Sea lo que sea
La vivienda es la
mejór vengánza-
Y si permites la opinion del
escritór.. Si a mí
me toca justícia
a puntilla,
Los pongo todos esos parásitos
en una fúnda
diréctamente mandada
gasolina koete nitro al
Sól! pero que bolúdos.

*Jose Gabriel Garcia*

## Política Y Cívilez en América

A los menos con la asisténcia
de la soledad,
se presenta un nido anudado.
En abundacia de opiniones
el nido nunca estás fuera del alcánce
De un bandido de ser vuerto;
argumentos que repíten
Témas sencillas sin correpondencia.
A los menos, de nuevo e ideálmente;
con la bendíta soledad se acompañas claridad de vista.

# Stolen/Theft

To successfully steal from a thief,
As goes the Caribbean saying,
grants one-hundred years of
Forgiveness and pardons;
The Hispañola banality can be
debilitating at the thought
but to think of the
pathetic cries and pleas in their storage closets
that would nauseate to the point of weakness- also brings to mind
that the heist would not even flow plain in the
slightest. Again though, it'd be up to the true victim
to sink into his will to fight!
for the pilferers, victims are like old and cold toast that gets buttered.

# Vacation

Aarrgh! not again-

In the name of love;

Spontaneous matching

sometimes known as puppy-love,

lust, curiosity

Culminating ultimately to love-lost.

By this time my heart is torn-

and beyond any known or foreseen

pleasant surprises.

I climbed, clawed, fought, drank, yelled, cursed;

Then staggered, walked, payed.

Morpheus, I need slumber.

When I wake, the beaconing forest stores my get-away from my

Gleaming gauntlet

To leave in a chest locked away.

My little Pandora's Box weighed along blissful moments...

The short drive to the forest is so meaningless my arrival at this forest is

no time at all.

When I pass the entrance to the forest

In-walking but I don't feel my footsteps.

In, moving effortlessly yet feeling my vigor. Bones aren't creaking though

and nerves aren't aching.

Ah and I approach irrelevant

gods touching on a subject so

distracting and alluring!

I chime in on my approach

Holding a laugh to see if any

of them understood.

Before I took my next breath

We all laughed in a circle

Some sitting, passing fruit and drink

A harp sounds o' so soft

so as to not interrupt

This serendipitous, sought after interim.

## Dripping Whet

That beer is stinking to be drunk.

Live one and it's done.

Try another one?

Do I?

Do I ever.!

# Experience and J. O'Barr's "The Crow"

"Fly slaughters".
[Wu-Tang]
reference to "fly" as-in, on the wall and
Take a hammer to it.

# My Second Community of Fish

The electricity in the air
The lingo in your lair
You're a happy bunch that make
Me happy.
That last addition of snails, is indeed
The last addition.
It has been a long day.

# Four Letter Words

Out of

The two-thousand-four-letter

Words I *can* think of-

I chose love.

Even amidst the barrage of hate

I may have gotten angry but I walked away.

Adjusting now,

This new year

Had its tumultuous pain.

This time the problem dissipated to old worries.

I can live, therefore I will.

The future years can guarantee

Far on in

For me alive.

I see a soul mutually satisfied.

Then.. for the proper hour

The trails I left

Will be the ones that mattered.

To everyone with care.

# Winter Night Sight

Looking through the glass where ice is collected.

At the bottom of the windowpane is a view of a small part of the

city.

On this clear moonless night where only a handful of the

brightest stars shimmering at extraordinary distances- with

the howling wind that constantly made its presence in the

abandoned ice covered streets with old footprints and tire

marks.

Nothing is untouched. The snow on the dark-gray

pavement illuminates the streets and the skies.

The warmer days I eagerly await.

# Summer Gone

After Spring
And it is as if You were never here.
Unusual Arctic Winters leave a dismal hope.
Cool flat sheets on a summer afternoon
Brings nostalgia to my senses!
A cool breeze that comes every so often.
The freedom to dress in less layers.
One is too many on some days..
There is of course the beach,
Of which I plan to make this year.
More reminiscing to the old days with old bids.
Maybe it will be just as fun this time around
multiplied by the not doings of last year.

# Fleeting Responses

The sketchbook
That is flipped through
With eleven and one half
Of its pages occupied.
Nothing concrete
or finished..
Must be new.

# Freudian Complex

The black road
Of my tears.
The black rose
Of my spite.
The orchid on the cliff.
(Sauntering)
And within my thoughts
Realize…
'Oh well, life could be hell'.
The blood red flower;
By the scene
Of my sights
in my visions..
A narrow trail sloping down the cliff
So inviting.
The oncoming night is but the spark to ignite
The strong curiosity to forgo
an undeniable continuum to infinitum.

## Dark Prayers

Vampire recounted
A prayer; A victim to
Become a blood-craver
that rejects Jesus from
the heart. Just as well;
I almost envied.

# Unmasked

Regarding-

degrees of pansyness.

Infectious scurrility spinning and weaving a set of threads

A camouflaged coffin.

Honor worthy future noble youngsters looking on-

At this potentially disastrous, foundationless, passive tantrum.

Other dudes on daylight hours will be decent taunt.

Something to mention after twilight.

'Else your pansy meter rises a notch of which would create a delay of game.

# Tired Hands

Communicatering-
and killing time.
Keeping my thoughts afloat
All awhile sinking in time.
Lightening my folks
around me's moods,
including mine own.
A chuckle, a smile.
I conquered the day.

# A Rap Star

Tupac Amaru Shakur,
Off Tupac's final shine, the Makiaveli'sz
The strands of independence
Find their way
Drip, dropping to...

## <u>Questioned Persuasions</u>

I'm saying the word to myself.
Visualizing it with my eyes closed.
Seeing something else,
Slightly
and it's a personal joke.
'tween me.. dna mi[h]-

# Questioned Persuasions II

Funny word it is, heh-heh-
Europe, in the pronunciation
And accent
Could be "you rope"
In print, change the "R" slightly and you have
"You Pope", and so-on, even!
No, not an easy discovery.

# Good Jokes

Again gone to waste, are they?..

Well, I'll tell you somethin'.

<u>This</u> one doesn't laugh

because he has a staged sense of humor.

<u>That</u> one does not budge because he's way too cool.

Then there's always the advice,

The critique,

The languid appraisal

Of the gold miners.

The gold diggers are already there.

They just don't see.

Some kind of bipolar validation.

All or nothing embedded in these peoples' heads.

Butter or shit.. yeeghk!

# Music

In the spectrum of music
There lies the sharp points
On the wound wheel which
Uses these spikes as percussion for
The sound the outstanding song makes.
Taking the creator at times.
When the particular song ends,
Twinging.. subsiding
You reflect on those times you bled.
When you remove your mandible off that percussion spike
A tune wound
Is imprinted in your mind.
The lyricists' mandibles are locked on that spike
When their life is lost
A curved metal does then locate that other end
To the wheel that turns.
Askance, with this broken band or deceased singer,
The wheel will turn.

# Beacon

On the bus stop

Hearing some kinda' tune.

Something happens when

I pass by cars on a stop-light.

On foot.

They turn off or

Tone down the music..

I look up the street

At the car in front at the stop light

And the music keep playing

He; because I know it is a "he" driving-

Looks like a beacon

In today's society.

When I get back home

I see I was letting in the winds.

Keepin' the piece.

Getting the receipts.

Later I saw when it went away

As you were watching it.

(smoke stack over black roof taken by the wind)

# Untitled

The way The Man
works.
The woman don't
respond.
You think it didn't happen?
Believe that.
Took your heart.

# High School Bud

Rain comes
fills the flower
If it stays strong
The sun will evaporate the goods.
Weak
And it will be eaten by the voracious
insects and dirt
when it makes that dramatic
fall.

*Inspired by Alcoholics Anonymous New Mexico

# Iron Flowers

The basking in the meadows
And running over hills
To finally stop panting and gasping for air, it is so fun.
A race through time with
Strangers, companions and God.
Recalling fallen strangers
Along then the companions fallen.
Iron flowers growing in the wild they are.
Untethered yet not always unkempt.
Gleefully gardenless
Only kept in the ruins of fondness and revere
Of our human existence.

# Civil Dreams

One bad day is o.k.
But when you are trying
to do your thing and it builds.
Being bred in the city
The small talk alludes to some getting used to.
Some fade like old edifices
To be shut down.
It is fun to walk by them in the night though;
once in a while.
So it's time to go home and take a godly shower
To be ready for my last hope of the would be fem.
In the meantime, she is so humble
On her way to me, so as when
She shows up in the bright lit
room, in a doorway
looking like a winter-stricken small tree
with plastic bags blowing attached to its limbs. The vivid
image from my dark room- whose snuffed lights seem not to invite her
nor turn her away.

The Sun is there in the morning.

Do you see the incongruity of this? Your "no"

Leaves you. Your fear is gruesomely obvious;

like gross coincidences

There is no taming a jungle,

So the drug option availability

To each individual their construction,

Like plastic carrying onzz.

Escape, joke, educate positively, dream! Fight reality.

# High Decibel

There is a sweet voice

On the other end.

When you hear a *man*

No matter what time of day,

it always sounds like they just let off one!

Right then and there...! All outrageously,

Scandalously into the nothingness.

I change my frequency

Making important pit stops

Frequently racing

my vehicle

Often growling

In the ubiquitousness where everything is everything,

subjectively taking driving serious without too much startling distraction

Is not difficult in our modern world-

Making it a fine getaway or miniature diversion.

# Living Garden

There once was a locked garden with strange flowers
Surrounded by grass with snakes roaming in them.
When the wind blew there was a chance
You'd see them or if you sat and focused.
In one corner there were snakes throwing hooks.
In the second corner there were snakes making love.
In the third corner there were snakes nursing eggs.
In the fourth corner there was a cactus and an ant hill.
If the wind blew soft enough
Over the garden appeared the optical illusion of an enticingly comfortable
empty bed.

# Out of Reach

My extremities disappear
As [she] majestically with
Simultaneous desires
glides approachingly.
Yet she leaves
Out of reach.

# Love

There are three essential
Types of social relationships
regardless of how insipid or maniacal.
Before I get to the good tips
it is only fair to say
Girls or females
like to play
Even the males
But I won't get into the dichotomy
Of who's dating what?
All I want to say
And point out is that
Befitted by watching eyes
very truly
There are those who loved
Those who have never loved
And those who have loved
And never will again.

# Forlorning

The hoes of yesterday, todays' former lovers and tomorrow's-
the past and at this hour:
Though my hopes are for my past woes
in all recurrences of memories or fitful dreams
wakefully metamorphose to a consoled
puffy cushioned orange leather booth
At a known pizza shop on a warm rainy evening.
Ducking the storm under awnings and
that refreshing odor the concrete has with the cool rains.
The parting clouds after
a surprising welcomed lifted storm
of nursed memories
Looking on to
on the way home crossing boulevard's, passing doorways
a probable perhaps every now and then on the way to dock for the day.
In constructing the next line
To have a sweet adventure-
In the passion of caress, moving conversations
Or culminating complete sex.

# Constipation

Snakes; for us humans with tubes & pipes,

May be the key to appreciation

Not destruction.

Doing away with disorderly existence

To get every possible machines at work..

Take care

Of the snake in your life;

There is a Dominican merengue that says,

"De todo un poco.." simply meaning, a little of everything..

Pain can sting. Pain from a snake can kill, so goes the law of the jungle.

Until of course the final bite, the bite of bites..

So be nice to your snake.

# Bewitched

Twilight hour.
Beer is gone.
Do I run out?

# Kneeling In Church

Paraphrased, Jesus said, you needn't go to church.

And being a naturalist yet a man of faith I asked myself,

What is the difference?

If one was to say to one's self,

"I truly am Satan",

Amidst the city sirens and the status-quo of emotions in

the way afternoon hours

You can always believe you really are.

Though as free thinking beings we can control our dedication to our deity.

Doing and not out doing

Existing positively in prayer and docilely.

Yet again though,

What be the difference if as free thinking beings

wrest of one's wonts is all equivalent to that what is perverse and trivial at most.

# The Fascinating Take

Musicians' music is

Poetry with rhythm and motion. And a silent poet

Has flawless poetic literature;

Both, in an as instrumentally

Unstammeringly perpetual crescendo

With enough at the end to keep you

Coming back; that is, the one that suits you.

If not it is a complete one hundred percent waste of time.

The fascinating take in music is many;

In literature I have one for you..

Howz this

When the American alphabet says 'Yes' it'll be the

end.

The transition to that will be another story, if even ever

told, I suppose.

# Constipataion: Version II

snakes; for us humans
as with forked tongues
Doing away with second questioning
mixed with biased thoughts.
The heart goes on.
Take control of your body first
yet simultaneously your mind
Inside then out.
Breathe.
Rise and rebellion
The ever battle.
Inside then out.
Inside. Then out.

# The Rams Curled Horns

The mingling in a forest
hornless for it isn't a ram (yet)
The power of the gods are-
Also roaming freely
Reality and myth were one and the
Same place.
The latter
Had the opportunity to
fade away and do so.
The gods had their eyes
On this large sheep
And taunted it and called it weak.
Worthy only
For sacrifice.
To the point where
This particular sheeps' feeling were hurt and it ran in
the direction of the voices.
The air was thick as it
Went forward.

The seamless fusion
Of reality and the other realm
And the large sheep
Took on a head-on collision
And the smooth impact
Curled and took form
Like a powerful wave of a storm.
This he took with him.
The border of both worlds.
Thus he became a Ram
and he said,
"You never had <u>me</u> fooled!"

*Jose Gabriel Garcia*

# Ephesian

I wake up
And see something big coming down
So I open and extend my arms
So as to see what it is and have it.
But only to realize my hands in chains,
And there is nothing in the sky.

# Biting Topics

Negative.

Positive.

Look at that dress, isn't [she] hot?

How about we drown that fly in soda?

Does anyone know how to pray, I read the instructions but

I still don't get it.

Ok.

That last one was crazy but you get the point.

Bob Marley's "Rebel".

That chorus is like turning around and facing a warm

light.

It takes you there.

Sober.

It takes you.

Negative.

Positive.

Clean up your room.

Clean the house.

Clean the car.

Clean yourself. Aw jeez.

Negative.

Positive.

The earth; All the mountains, the blue oceans,

The streams, all- all of it.

Drowning.

Falling.

Running.

Lifting.

Hitting.

Cutting.

Negative.

Positive..

# Tense Talk

Depending on who you're talking to
Whether it be yourself or another
'bout pressures or recreation
Communication can be so informative
Negative or positive and personal.
Speaking of the present-tense of the future tense
Communicative contact will never die.
As long as the world turns,
Like a deck of cards it can be shuffled
and dealt for a new set of patterns.
Past tense can have those of the deceased
Mistakes you have made from and good memories
The past of which is every split second
Lost.
The present appreciation
The future to be gained.

# <u>Safe House for the Traveling Nun</u>

On a very quiet night in a forest not well known to civilization, long ago.. when superstition ran rampant and things like today's modern industry was a far cry to common knowledge, there was a nun with an important package to deliver. To deliver this package she had to cross the sparse old forest that night.

The Sister was well on her way from the convent and took note on how the twilight was heavenly mercy revealing to her the widening forest as she trekked along. Trees were well apart. Seemingly out of respect for each other's personal growing space or perhaps cared for by genius green-thumb and landscaper.

She followed the dusty down trodden road hurrying trying to remember the directions told her before she left her home.

When night approached the trees lining the road, along with intermittent trees further off the road, lit, with huge lightning bugs. The lamps were constructive containers assisted to nature for the traveler at night on this path. These lamps drew tree sap and nutrients that attracted all kinds of insects. So when the lightning bugs entered the container it served as their buffet. For the night traveler it served as a guide not to swerve off the unpaved road; even at the lamps strobe, following the path wasn't too difficult.

This particular sister was dressed traditionally and wore only a large cross necklace for her protection. The cross was simply decorated. It was black stone lined with silver and Corinthian-like ends. As she tread on through the forest she could see small white dots appearing deep in the forest night between the large spaces the young trees in the forest had had. The dots would then disappear only to reappear again in a manner she could tell was unusual. She had heard stories of monsters and werewolves lurking in this forest. This startled our brave nun so she picked up the pace three fold and thought that perhaps she'd be able to make it to the next stop post and wait until morning. The resting stop was blessed with all that is Holy keeping away unwelcomed beasts or outsiders. Although not manned the spirit of the forest agreed to have the Church of Christ bless the old path and the rest-stops. This truce occurred right before the hostile beasts would make their way to the other convent unpassable via the dirt road. Hence, the dotted points in the forest were strategic to save lives for those caught traveling after dark.

As she kept her pace steady she was about to pass a tree and tripped on one of the roots. Before she hit the ground a limb swung around and grabbed her around the waist. There appeared a pair of dark green stern eyes at the trunk of the tree and there was come a voice with no mouth. A mist started to blanket the forest around her and quickly thickened as well. The tree asked her "Where are you off to? There are beasts some of which I have come to recognize only their wails. Beasts including werewolves. Creatures savage enough to make a meal out of you". She answered, "I have a parcel to deliver to the convent at the other end of this path, just outside the forest". To this the tree said, "You won't make it to even the safe-house down the road, of which is still some miles away. I can give you two choices: let me help you for a small price or keep traveling at your risk. The nun took only seconds to respond, "What is the price you ask for your help?" The tree narrowed its stare and said with a thinner branch toying with the nun's necklace, "This trinket we will barter for your safe reach to your convent." The tree removed the silver laced cross necklace around her neck and with the limb holding her lowered her with the thick mist clouding around her where she vanished, parcel and all. The green eyes dimmed shut and only bark on the trunk remained. The tree resumed the unassuming uprightness and the nun's necklace the black onyx cross fell next to it. Only the silver lining around the cross, the most ornate accent of it, could be seen from the glowing lamps now and again.

# My Home Town

My home town is New York City. It took some time for me to realize New York City never sleeps. At a young age education and knowledge centers seemed to be everywhere. Even the most rebellious of kids sought somewhere to learn what appealed to them. Upper Manhattan has the Harlem River Drive and there in a river walk where the perceptive eye can see how the city is built around and works with nature. The greenhouse effect had little affect on the infrastructure and masonry but winters became bitterly cold.

Manhattan is the smallest island county in the world and yet it is the capital of the world. This alone says much of my learning experiences and to my eventually coming of age. I received schooling in untampered American History, fundamentals of physics and in literature of all kinds. Inspirational teachers or educational radio shows were a major motivational influence.

The part of town I grew up in is so awesome! After traveling around town with my mom, whether for shopping or visiting someone in the winter, when we returned to our neighborhood and were heading home we realized the temperature was a bit warmer. The elevation in our neighborhood, I then came to notice was lower than most if not all of the rest of Manhattan County. After experiencing this welcoming phenomenon most years than not my theory is that from the start of the lower elevation Northward the neighborhood was warmed by the waters of the river from the Sun and then to the cold breeze until of course sundown.

Winters from that time of my childhood were often snow laden, packed up three to four feet. When rains would shower the city in the fall, cold waters gradually

turned to cold winds and cold nights. As the late seventies went on to the late eighties, global warming seemed to take an obvious effect on New York's climate. The four seasons were reduced to perhaps three: Spring, summer and winter. Spring was colder than normal with the struggling blossoms. Summers have been shortened to late June through early September. Winters have adopted global warming out of the rest of the other three seasons. Snow falls have lessened; wind-chill factors duration mutated drastically, lowering temperatures throughout the winter.

Friends and helping hands have made the best of hard times and difficult changes.

My hometown is New York City. It took some time for me to realize New York City never sleeps. Education played a role in my childhood and inspiring literature I sought out and successfully found always surprised me somehow. The bustling streets remain a far cry from the tranquility of the libraries. Flash flood rains have stopped all public transportation and extreme heat has occasionally taken elderly lives. Those are signs of change in the environment that are no longer gradual but harsh and extreme. The people of the city make the city.

That is why

I love New York.

# Mi Amor, Mi Lupa

In our seizful,
wrested from time escaping-
Ever challenging,
we stare at us and
you bring forth from me
Those long ago playful
instinctual techniques
that, self taught, I
used to appreciate.
The spectrum of beauty-
your words to me
my words to you
In all reflection of our minds truly viewing each other.
This once forgotten
Coalescence turned into defense
Is renewed, brushed off-
Every last dark speckle.

We are making ourselves better
around each other all of our individualness
¡Te como a puro besos!
Through the waning day
the dew that we percolate,
revolving-togetherness love,
rolls on the salmon petal.
the shade of the median
gradiating perfect light in translucence
Meeting the curling edge.

# One Moment In Time

One moment in time
reached through space
validating all Pain.
And all life
stood still. For in
this breath in
this one blink of
an eye.
There was only
You!!
Only Me!!
Just US!!
I love you Jose so
much the I can't put
into words. I miss you
A lot a lot a lot of the
time. Thank you mi *amor*
for you! My handsome
Sexy everyday Valentine.

# Natural Impressions

O' tree

You are so innocent

Just like me

Rough

Strong

Rooted

We have a fair trade —even-

Thought you are more innocent

Heavenly

You must be observing me

O' tree I love you every which way!

## One Day

I felt your encouragement
When I saw your radiance
Upon the ice and snow~
In the frigid air
trying so hard so warm
But it belongs to the season
Yours will come soon.

# The Old Days

Bridging customs to where will my life leadz. To have, receive or gets me
what I needz. Is solidarity, in the environment with my
little
house in the middle of nowhere, with tons of vegetation,
streams, rivers, lakes at the far end, with nothing- anything
else as a useless option. That is all I needz right now. I
know where it will leadz… Happily Ever After!

# Antenna Itch

There was a kid on Christmas who received from
his
father a special walkie-talkie set
that fit on with an ear piece.
It could lock into other coordinates
and talk to others on walkie-talkies.
The boy was nine years of age.
Other than talkying with his father,
he had many conversations on happenstance with strangers
Around the world.
So he would hear problems of the world by people
worse off than himself
For example, even those better off but not happy
for some reason or another.
The kid believed in God and asked himself
where's God in all of this.
So he tried a different frequency on his walkie-
talkie dial
and spoke into it, "God, God do you copy?"

# Untitled

At a prerecorded live event introducing new gadgets
the "Chap Saver" is displayed on stage and
in the audience the big cats have arrived late for a seating
greeting and getting around one another one can overhear
'Leopard-on; Jaguár you?; Lynx-o where is the Ocelot and the rest of the
aristocrats; did the sent out invitations have the gathering hour incorrect?'

# A Spinning Cog

Butterfly
Roses and hammers
for the butterfly..
Butterfly
Chisel and hammers
for the butterfly.
The confessor and the concenter. Concurror.

Printed in the United States
by Baker & Taylor Publisher Services